MEDITATION

THE ESSENTIAL BOOK OF

MEDITATION

—

How to harness
the power of inner
reflection

TARA WARD

SIRIUS

In memory of my sister-in-law, Barbara Sullivan,
a sweet soul who is loved and missed by many.

All images courtesy of Shutterstock.

SIRIUS

This edition published in 2021 by Sirius Publishing, a division of
Arcturus Publishing Limited,
26/27 Bickels Yard, 151–153 Bermondsey Street,
London SE1 3HA

ISBN: 978-1-3988-1343-4
AD010178UK

Printed in China

Contents

What is Meditation?

Why have you picked up this book? Perhaps you know a little about meditation and like the sound of it. Perhaps you often feel that life must be something more than working, eating and sleeping.

Through meditation you can learn to enjoy every single moment of the life you have at present, to acknowledge and appreciate everything that is working well for you and to turn negative scenarios into positive, encouraging ones.

Meditation has been described as 'deep reflection'. By becoming calm and silent and slowly withdrawing our senses from the world, we can reflect on anything and everything in a much more profound way. The deeper the reflection, the more we are likely to learn from it. The secret lies in how well we can learn to withdraw.

Meditation is a wonderful opportunity to work on your ability to focus and concentrate. It is possible to shut out distractions and irritations through learning to meditate.

VOYAGE OF DISCOVERY

One of the many joys of meditation is that it is utterly personal to you and no one else can totally share your experience. What is doubly wonderful about meditation is that it is absolutely free and can be practised entirely in your own time!

Meditation is also more than this. It's about going quietly within to work out more about yourself and others on a deeper level. This then opens up a wealth of benefits.

It means we can learn to accept ourselves exactly as we are. It means we can understand why we are where we are in life and what we might do to shift areas of our life that appear 'stuck'. The simple exercises coming up will show you the way forward with this.

Embrace silence

A re you someone who finds silence unnerving? We have become so used to constant noise that shutting it out altogether can be unsettling. Do you always have the radio or some music on, either at home, at work or when you travel? Are you used to the sounds of people talking constantly, of traffic outside your windows, or of a neighbour's dog barking frequently? Start to notice what sounds are around you constantly.

How often do you enjoy the natural sounds of nature around you? Are you aware of bird song? Can you hear the wind rustling in the trees or the whooshing of a fast-flowing stream or brook? Are there any natural sounds that you can enjoy on a regular basis, either near your home or work place? If not, think about taking a trip to a park or the seaside and enjoying the peace that it affords.

SWITCH OFF

Try switching off the radio, television or stereo system. Let yourself experience the silence. How does it make you feel? Sometimes we actually want distracting sounds around us because we don't want to be quiet. We are afraid to sit still because we fear that we might end up thinking about lots of issues that we've been trying to push into the background.

In other words, we often use sounds as a means of covering up how we are really feeling. If you know that you do this, don't worry. Meditation will gently and gradually reveal to you that you needn't be afraid of any of those emotions and worries. It can teach you to let go and release the anxieties blocking your way forward. If you are someone who relishes silence and loves the feeling of peace that it affords you, then you are well on your way to enjoying meditation!

Focus on awareness

The early stages of meditation involve appreciation of what is around us. Try this simple exercise involving an item of food to work on your senses.

Choose a simple food that you are happy to eat. It can be something as simple as a single grape or a sugar cube. Hold it in your hand and look at it.

Where has it come from? Do you know anything about the manufacture of this item? Think about all the components that went into this item in your hand. Nature must have played a part somewhere, if it was grown. Rain and sun were important at one stage.

What about the people who either picked this item or put it together or worked the machines that manufactured it? How did you get it to where you are now?

Consider the item in your hand. It actually has had quite a journey to make it to you. Now, say a silent 'thank you' to everyone who participated in this journey from raw state to finished product. Acknowledge that everything around you has gone through a similar journey. How does that make you think and feel?

SAVOUR THE MOMENT

Now eat the item, slowly, with awareness and appreciation. Notice how you feel while eating it. Is it different from how you would have felt if you had simply popped it into your mouth without stopping to think about it?

If it was a natural item, did you feel more drawn to eat it? If it was a processed item, did you feel less inclined to want to consume it? Appreciation of everything is a far more powerful and all-encompassing act than you might first suppose. This exercise is an example of meditation as an everyday, vibrant part of living.

Part One
And Breathe...

"Our minds can accomplish extraordinary tasks that often defy logical thought."

Learning to breathe

You might find this title odd. Surely you already know how to breathe! It's something you've been doing quite successfully on your own since you were born, usually unconsciously.

Yet how much do you know about your own breathing? The majority of the time, we simply breathe in and out unconsciously and constantly, without ever stopping to think about it. Do you know what is physically happening to your body every time you breathe in and out? Have you any idea of the beauty and complexity of your breathing system?

It is through awareness of our breathing that we access every meditative state. Every human breathes every minute of every day, on average about 15 times per minute. However, how often are you aware of your breathing? How often do you notice each breath coming in and going out? The answer is probably almost never! So meditating is about awareness of the breath. Just as we discussed in the previous chapter about meditating being awareness and appreciation of everything, so awareness of your own breathing is the key to learning how to meditate.

Most of us also don't breathe deeply and fully. Meditation is about learning how to breathe deeply into the lungs, enjoying every single in and out movement, rejoicing in the power and beauty of our own breathing system. This close observation of our own breath allows us to slip effortlessly into a deeper state of relaxation and thereby enjoy a true meditative state. The process really is as basic as that. However, learning how to truly observe your breath and to focus solely on that is not quite as easy as it first sounds.

How do we breathe?

The reason we don't tend to breathe properly is the result of an under-used muscle just below our lungs called the diaphragm. Every time we breathe in, the diaphragm flattens out, to allow the lungs to fill up with air. When we breathe out again, the diaphragm assumes the shape of an inverted 'U', helping to squeeze the last of the air out of our lungs. This process is then repeated every time we breathe in and out.

ARE YOU DOING IT RIGHT?

Most of us don't use the diaphragm properly. We tend to go around doing what is called shallow breathing. This means we fill the top part of our lungs with air, but not the bottom two thirds and thus, as the diaphragm is resting on the bottom of the lungs, it is never used fully. Certain professions are exceptions to this. Opera singers and athletes are people who have to learn to breathe deeply. Musicians who play wind instruments also come into this category, as do stage actors. Anyone can learn how to breathe deeply; it simply takes a little practice.

How do you know if you are breathing deeply or not? Below is a simple exercise to check what is happening with you.

Stand in front of a mirror that shows you the top half of your body, down to your waist. Take a deep breath in and notice if your shoulders lift as you do so. Can you see them rising? If you can, then you are doing what is called shallow breathing. You are filling the top half of your lungs but not the remainder. Don't worry if this is the case for you.

Testing your diaphragm

S tand in front of your mirror. Place your hands over the lower part of your ribcage so that your middle fingers are just touching. Now take a good, deep breath in. Let your ribcage slowly and comfortably expand.

Have your fingertips moved apart just a little? If they have, you are learning to breathe deeply. If they haven't, breathe out and then take a breath in again, but this time watch your shoulders and upper chest. Are they rising again? If so, remember that you are breathing only into the top of your lungs and not further down.

Focus on your lower ribcage again. Don't force your breath but simply imagine all the air coming in and going down into the lower part of your lungs. Let your ribcage expand outward. Are your fingertips moving just a little bit apart now?

Strengthening your diaphragm

Sometimes just focusing on your fingertips can seem a discouraging business, as no matter how hard you focus the ribcage doesn't seem to want to expand any distance. There are various techniques you can use to help deepen your breathing. Several exercises are detailed below and you might want to practise these on a regular basis for a number of weeks. But remember, if you start to feel dizzy, stop. Resume your normal breathing and don't return to the exercise for at least fifteen minutes.

These exercises basically use a thought process to allow you to breathe fully without any effort. Our mind or imagination can accomplish extraordinary tasks that often defy logical thought. You probably notice this when day dreaming. Some people can simply close their eyes and effortlessly transport themselves somewhere else, even smelling the scents and being aware of a different atmosphere.

Stomach breathing

Many people find the following exercise quite liberating. It breaks with the conventional way of teaching breathing, and by concentrating on something you know isn't true, it becomes an enjoyable game rather than a difficult task to focus on.

Sit down in a comfortable upright chair, close your eyes and focus on your breathing. Don't try to do anything with the breath, just observe it coming in and going out. You will notice some breaths are naturally shorter than others, some seem longer. Don't try to force your breathing into any regular pattern. Just enjoy observing it.

TRY THIS

* Now we're going to play a game. Next time you breathe in, imagine that your lungs are actually down in your stomach. You know that they aren't, that they rest under your ribcage, but, just for fun, let's pretend they are under your navel. Enjoy the sensation of the breath going all the way down into your stomach. Remember not to force it, just let the warm air float all the way down to your stomach area. Follow the path of the breath back up again, from your stomach, all the way up and out through your nose again. Notice how much warmer the out breath is after the inside of your body has warmed it. Keep repeating this process for a few minutes.

* Remember you are not trying to breathe deeply during this, you are simply redirecting your breath to another area of your body. Don't force anything. Let the air come and go naturally and easily but keep focusing on the thought that your lungs are in your stomach.

* After a few minutes, take the focus away from your stomach and let your breathing return to normal.

Balloon breathing

This exercise is another useful way of playing with your breathing and not trying to force yourself to breathe more deeply. The moment we focus on something in an intense, uncomfortable way, we create all sorts of blocks to breathing deeply and fully.

TRY THIS

✳ Sit in a comfortable upright chair and close your eyes. Start to focus on your breathing but do not direct it in any way. Let your breath come and go naturally without forcing it. Enjoy the freedom of observing your breath without trying to control it.

✳ Now imagine that your lungs have ten little balloons inside them, five in each lung. They are tough balloons with thick skins that won't burst. The next time you breathe in, notice how many of the balloons are being blown up. Are they all inflating? If they are, increase the number of balloons in each lung. If only a few of the balloons have been half-inflated, then reduce the number to whatever feels manageable. You do not want to make this exercise hard work; it should be enjoyable.

✳ Now you want to help blow up all your balloons. Take a deep comfortable breath in and notice how the balloons fill up, easily and effortlessly. Breathe out and watch them deflate again. Does it feel as though they are all working properly? Keep focusing on the balloons in your lungs and keep expanding your breath, easily and effortlessly, until you feel all the balloons inflating and deflating comfortably with each in and out breath.

✳ Then let the image of the balloons fade. Return to your normal, shallow breathing. After a few minutes, open your eyes and focus on an item in the room. Make sure you have returned fully to normal breathing before you stand up.

Ribcage breathing

Once you start to discover the joys of breathing deeply, it becomes a pleasure to let yourself slip into that relaxed state, and it becomes something you can do easily and effortlessly. This is another simple exercise to improve breathing deep into your lungs.

TRY THIS

✳ Sit in a comfortable upright chair and close your eyes. Start off by watching your breath as it goes in and out. Don't force it in any way, just let it come and go naturally. Sometimes it's shallow, sometimes the breath seems longer and deeper. Let it be and simply observe how it feels. Take your time.

✳ Now you want to think about your ribcage. Notice on the next breath in, how the ribcage slowly expands outwards. Notice as you breathe out, how the ribcage contracts back into the body again. Keep observing this movement of the ribcage without trying to alter it in any way.

✳ Next, you want to imagine that every time your ribcage expands, it is actually reaching further and further outwards. Keep your eyes closed as you do this. You know your ribcage isn't really extending out into the room, but play with your imagination and feel as though it is. Gradually have it expand, without trying to make it happen. Know your thoughts are simply having fun. There is no effort involved. Even have your ribcage touch the walls of the room you are in! Imagine your ribcage as soft and free flowing. See it billowing out around the room, effortlessly expanding and contracting. Notice how it seems to have a life of its own, easy and unrestricted. Play with this new freedom for a while.

✳ When you are ready, return to your normal breathing, and as you do so let the image of your expanding ribcage fade. If you have really lost yourself in this game and want to come back to reality, simply place your hands either side of your ribcage. Recognise how solid and real your ribcage is now. Open your eyes and gaze at an object in the room. Wait a few minutes before standing up.

Alternate nostril breathing

Based on yogic techniques, alternate nostril breathing is a simple but incredibly powerful technique that helps to calm, ground and focus your thoughts. You won't appreciate how well this works until you experience it for yourself.

TRY THIS

❊ Close your eyes. Place your right hand over your face so that your thumb can close off your right nostril and your little finger and the finger next to it can comfortably close the left nostril. Your index and middle fingers can rest lightly against your forehead.

❊ Now you are going to close off your right nostril and breathe in through your left nostril. Close your left nostril and breathe out through your right nostril. Still keeping your left nostril closed, breathe in again through your right nostril. Close off your right nostril. Breathe out through your left nostril. Still keeping your right nostril closed, breathe in again through your left nostril and then repeat the process. After a little while you will find it is easy to get into a comfortable rhythm.

✳ As you follow the pattern, count to two slowly as you breathe in and then again as you breathe out. Gradually increase this to four as you breathe in and four as you breathe out. Once you can breathe in and out comfortably to the slow count of four, you can introduce a pause between each in and out breath. Count to two slowly in these pauses.

IN SUMMARY

Breathe in through left nostril to count of four

Hold for two

Breathe out through right nostril to count of four

Hold for two

Breathe in through right nostril to count of four

Hold for two

Breathe out through left nostril to count of four

Hold for two

Part Two
Mini Meditations

'The only thing that is
absolutely definite and real
is this actual moment.'

What are mini meditations?

Now you have had a good introduction to breathing and what it really entails, we're going to start looking at how you can incorporate short meditations into every aspect of your daily life and the benefits this can bring you.

Mini meditations are quite quick, don't involve a lot of deep concentration and the amazing results they offer can give you just the boost you need to encourage you into the deeper realms of more prolonged meditations.

As always, with all the exercises in this book, taking a moment to breathe freely and deeply is important every single time you prepare for a meditation, whether it is for a very brief, mini meditation or a meditation lasting for an hour or more. Your breathing is always the key to the door of possibility.

FINDING PURPOSE IN DAILY TASKS

A good way to describe these quick techniques would be as a moment of appreciation and awareness. They can encompass anything, from an item of food (as, for example, the food appreciation exercise we did in the first chapter) to an inanimate object, an animal or a person. A mini meditation can relate to an action you are taking, even something as simple as walking down the road. It can be done as you wash the dishes, do some shopping or sit at your desk at work. A mini meditation is a short period of time that you use to reflect upon something. That something does not have to be deeply profound. You can find a purpose, meaning and good use in everything in daily life, if you want to.

Waking-up meditation

L et's start with something many people find a chore: getting up in the morning. Do you find this difficult? If motivating yourself to get up is hard work, take a few minutes after waking to work through the following:

Lie still in bed for a moment. Resist the urge to shut off to everything and take a few deep breaths. Tell yourself you will not sleep. Instead of focusing on what you don't like about getting up, what can you find to appreciate about this moment?

TRY THIS

Here are a few suggestions (not all of them may apply to you but consider those which do):

* You have spent the night in a comfortable bed

* You have had a rejuvenating sleep

* You live in a prosperous country, free from war

* You have a job to go to

＊ You have friends and family who love you

＊ You have your health

＊ Something wonderful may happen to you today

＊ You have water to wash in and food to eat

＊ You have clothes to put on your body

＊ You are alive

Choose just one statement relevant to you and let your thoughts focus on it. Remember to keep breathing deeply and easily. What happens when you focus on one of these aspects of your life? Do you find yourself floating back into the negative with 'Ah, yes, but…'? Pull your thoughts back and focus on what you can appreciate now.

When you are ready, give silent thanks for what you have got and then get out of bed, resolving to allow yourself brief moments of awareness when you will appreciate what is in your life right now.

Good health meditation

Think of when you have been ill, say with a bad dose of the flu. Can you remember how dreadful you felt and the incredible relief when you started to feel better and memory of the illness faded? That time when you realised you were feeling better was quite wonderful, wasn't it? Can you remember the enormous relief and sense of appreciation you felt when you knew you were improving? Try to recall that sensation of overwhelming gratitude and pleasure. For that moment, could you not tangibly experience how all of you felt alive, grateful and content?

However, once you recovered, did you have any lingering sense of appreciation for your good health? Did you go around daily feeling good about the fact that you were healthy and full of energy? Perhaps you did for a day, maybe half a day. Then your life no doubt returned to its usual routine and you forgot to appreciate your current state of health. That is, until you fell ill again and the cycle started to repeat itself!

What might our lives be like if we spent all of our time living in a state of appreciation for what we had, constantly remembering all the positive qualities around and in us? What if every day we focused on what was good and took the time to appreciate everyone and everything around us? For example, how do you think you would feel if you spent the majority of your time acknowledging your good health and were aware of the pleasure and peace stemming from it?

Smiling meditation

Did you know that smiling relaxes about a hundred muscles in your face? Many of us hold so much tension there throughout each day – a smile will release that tension. Also, there is now proof that breaking into a smile actually sets off certain chemical reactions in our body that tells our brain we are happy. In other words, the simple process of smiling can make us feel better.

Think of a difficult or stressful situation. Let yourself feel the emotion for a moment. Notice you will not want to smile! Give yourself a moment or two to worry and feel gloomy about what is happening. Look around the room you are in and notice things. Are they depressing, negative things you pick up on? Really allow yourself to feel the stress. Notice how it affects your body, your breathing, your mental and emotional state. Now choose to let it go. Let the worrying issue recede. Feel it fade into the distance. Take a moment to accomplish this. Notice if you find it hard to let go.

FEEL JOY

Now, think of something that makes you happy, something that makes you feel really good. Smile. Let it become a big, generous smile. How does it make you feel? Notice the changes you feel inside: physically, emotionally and mentally. Allow yourself to feel happy and appreciative of what you have. Look around you, wherever you are right now. How does everything seem? Can you suddenly see something nice that you hadn't appreciated before? Let yourself rest in that state for a moment. Keep smiling. You may have the feeling of well-being increase and swell inside and around you. Enjoy the moment. When you're ready, stop smiling, but retain that feeling of comfort and happiness you discovered inside.

Being in the now

Most of us have trouble with this concept of enjoying each moment as it exists. We tend to live more with our thoughts in the future, or sometimes in the past, if we feel either state is preferable to the present. We want to learn how to live 'in the now' and enjoy it.

A lot of people don't really understand the concept of enjoying every moment as it comes along, because they are naturally so geared up to believing life is about planning for the future and thinking ahead. Perhaps it is to do with affording another child or a bigger house or planning for retirement. Everything becomes about the future.

Yet the future doesn't exist. It hasn't happened yet. You have no guarantees about what will happen to you. You also can't change anything in your past. The only thing that is absolutely definite and real is this actual moment.

FINDING VALUE

What positive changes might we be able to make if we clearly see everything around us now and take full advantage of it to shape our future? So, if we can obtain greater awareness and understand better how to find our intended path in life through being 'in the now', how can we achieve that state? We can do it by constantly undertaking mini meditations that remind us who and what we are and how valuable everything we do is, no matter how slight or trivial it may seem.

Consider the routines that you carry out on a daily basis, and see how you can give them more meaning and purpose. What other things do you do that you would classify as a chore, without any joy attached to them? Most people would agree that house-cleaning, clothes-washing and shopping are boring. So how can we transform them?

Shopping meditation

Start your awareness about shopping by carefully considering what you put on your shopping list. Do you really need all the items you are writing down? How much of the food listed is actually healthy and will fill you with energy and nurture your body?

Now consider where you want to shop. What businesses would you like to support? Whose ethics do you value? You want to walk into that store with a smile on your face, happy to give custom to the people involved.

Do you want to avoid genetically modified food? Do you prefer organic produce? Do you care that the food you eat is ethically produced without 'slave' labour or unfair regulations? Which countries would you like to support by buying their produce? What ingredients are harmful in the detergents we use today? What can you do about this?

These are all very searching questions, and you may feel daunted by some of them. Remember it doesn't have to happen all at once. Make small changes.

Notice, when you do your shopping, how differently you feel. Realise that you can acknowledge and bless the people involved in the chain of actions that brings you the products you buy, starting with those who oversaw the creation of the raw ingredient right the way through to the person who sold you the final product.

As you walk around the different shops and acknowledge the wealth of produce available to you, remember others who have so little or virtually nothing. Take the time to send them a prayer of love and support. Awareness of others is the starting point of compassion. Without initial awareness, we will not act.

Turn the simple act of shopping into a completely aware 'meditation' of seeing what is happening here and now and using it to reassess how you want to live your life.

Rubbish-awareness meditation

There is nothing in life that can't be transformed into a positive action or emotion, if your attitude is that you are seeking true awareness of a situation. As an ultimate test, how about being aware of emptying your own rubbish? Try this exercise next time you empty out the rubbish.

For one week, before you throw anything into your bin, think about what you are planning to put into it. How much of what you throw away could be recycled?

Have you ever thought about starting a compost heap with your vegetable and fruit parings?

Do you need to use all the plastic products you have at present? Can you refill certain bottles or cut down on items that aren't strictly necessary?

SAVING THE PLANET

With every item you prepare to throw away, be aware of any use it might be put to. Can an empty jam jar become a container for something? Is that houseplant really dead or could you take a cutting and have it regrow into a strong, new plant?

When you have assessed that everything in your bin really needs to be there, notice how much smaller the amount has become as a result of your awareness.

Notice how the awareness of what is rubbish and what isn't makes you rethink your lifestyle, how you eat and how you live. Apart from helping you to reassess your own needs, it is enabling you to shift your perception of the whole planet.

If you know that you are creating the minimum of waste, you know that you are doing your bit to help the planet and reduce our increasing pollution problem. One of the benefits of acting with awareness is that it affords you a greater sense of inner peace through acting responsibly and carefully.

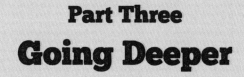

Part Three

Going Deeper

'Meditation is often described as being about the discovery of an inner peace and stillness.'

Preparing for meditation

While mini meditations don't require any preparation, apart from taking the time to focus on awareness and breathing, when we work at a deeper level it is important to adhere to guidelines that are there to nurture and protect you.

So what are we going to be doing next and why do we have to prepare ourselves for it in a certain way? Meditation is often described as being about the discovery of an inner peace and stillness. With mini meditations, this sense is not as pronounced. You were working much more on an external level of appreciation and awareness. To go within and to discover a profound stillness and peace requires another level of concentration and prolonged focus. You need to ease yourself into this new experience by giving consideration to a number of external aids that will help you.

Take a look at the following list. This should be your check list for all future meditations. It's important that you follow each of the actions, especially in the early stages of learning to meditate. In the chapter ahead you can work through each point and look at why it is necessary. Awareness of what each action entails will allow you to accept each condition and to enjoy working with it, rather than fighting against it.

YOUR CHECKLIST

○ A quiet, undisturbed location

○ Wear loose, comfortable clothing

○ Be alcohol and drug free

○ A comfortable position in which
   you can sit/lie completely still

○ Cleanse before you start meditating

○ Remember to breathe!

○ Place a glass of water within easy reach

A quiet undisturbed location

This is essential. To access the wonderful world of inner awareness requires a degree of concentration. You can't concentrate if you are constantly being interrupted. You must have a quiet space where no one can disturb you. If you can't trust someone not to come in, such as an animal or young child, then make sure you can lock the door. Put on the answerphone, switch off your mobile phone, make sure everything is geared towards your not being interrupted. Make sure other people in the building know that you do not want to be disturbed.

Another reason for a finding a quiet space is that some meditations leave you feeling emotional afterwards; this might take the form of a 'high' or euphoria, or you might find yourself feeling quiet and subdued, needing to mull over the insights you received during meditation. Whatever your state, you may feel vulnerable for a while and want to be alone to rebalance yourself before facing the external world again. These sensations are normal and common.

Creating a sacred space

So what makes a good meditation 'room'? Not everyone has the luxury of being able to create their own private space. If you only have the option of a bedroom or study, you will already have certain decor that you will probably not want to change. It doesn't matter in the sense that you can meditate anywhere, as long as it is private and you will be undisturbed.

If you do have a choice and there is a room you can have to yourself, then the key to a meditation room can be summed up in one word: simplicity. You want to create a space that is conducive to you slipping quietly into inner peace and awareness.

What symbolises peace to you? Most people would say white or pale pastel colours. The plainer the room the less likely you are to be distracted by the things in it.

Perhaps you might want to add something that is spiritual for you. This might be a representative of nature such as a vase of fresh flowers, a beautiful stone or piece of driftwood. Perhaps you prefer a painting or poster of a rainbow, body of water or a forest.

If you are fortunate enough to have your own space to decorate (and it need only be very small, just big enough for you to sit in comfortably), then give serious consideration to the few items you put in there. Sit in awareness in your room for a while and let your own wisdom come to you and show you what is right for this space. The simpler the better.

Wear soft, loose clothing

This may seem quite unimportant but the fact is that you want to help yourself in every way possible to sit quietly and relax into your meditation. There are always things to distract you as you start to focus on your breathing and uncomfortable clothing is an easy diversion. Anything that cuts into the neck or waist stops you from focusing on your breath. Avoid a fabric that is scratchy or makes you feel claustrophobic, but also make sure you are warm enough. As no one else will see you when you meditate, this is your time to relax and to be exactly as you want to be.

Wear those really baggy trousers that are loose around the waist, put on that stained jumper which is so soft and warm. You are not going to enter a fashion show, you are just going to be yourself in a totally relaxed state, so you might as well make the most of it.

It's best not to wear anything on your feet whilst meditating. You want to be as unrestricted as possible. The feet are also useful as a means of grounding yourself when you bring yourself back to reality afterwards, and it's easier to feel grounded without footwear.

Think about colours too. Do you find certain colours more soothing than others? If you find bright red stimulating, it might not be a good choice for clothing as you meditate.

If you find you are drawn to particular clothing when you practise meditation, then keep them purely for that purpose. No one else needs to see you in them and you can be comfortable and cosy in your own space.

Avoid drugs and alcohol

This is a must. Alcohol and drugs do not mix with meditation. Even one glass of wine or a strong headache tablet can set your mind working in a way that is not remotely compatible with altered states of awareness. Never, ever drink or take drugs and then try to meditate.

Why is this so important? One of the experiences you may have during meditation is a sense of being protected, nurtured and guided by other energies around you. It manifests itself as a faint but lovely feeling of warmth and comfort that slowly comes over you and permeates your body. It is a great joy when this happens and once you've experienced it, you can't wait for the next time. Alcohol and drugs distort the mind which can have an unsettling effect and is the opposite of feeling protected and nurtured.

It is also easier not to meditate with a full stomach as you will find yourself constantly being diverted in thought towards your rather heavy and bloated stomach. A light meal is better. Preferably, though, wait several hours after eating before you meditate.

Get comfortable

To enter a deeper meditative state, you want to try to maintain a motionless, comfortable position. This may not always be possible, but it is your aim.

Sitting in a straight-backed chair, with your hands resting comfortably on your lap with palms facing up, is a great way to meditate as your body is in natural alignment. It's best if you can keep a right angle between your upper and lower legs and for your upper legs to be parallel to the floor. Again, this is to place as little strain on your body as possible. If you need to sit on a thicker cushion, or even put something like pile of books under your feet to make this work, then it's a good idea to do so.

If you want to experiment with lying down for meditation, lie flat on your back, with your legs stretched out and a distance apart. Your arms should rest straight out on the floor and a foot or so away from your body with the palms facing upwards. Your head should be in a straight line to the rest of your body and you should be looking up at the ceiling. This position puts least strain on your body, whilst allowing it to be in alignment. The main problem with lying down is that it is so tempting to go to sleep, particularly if you are tired!

If for whatever reason neither of these positions is comfortable for you, don't worry. It is the fact that you have a clear intention of learning how to meditate that is of paramount importance. Although certain positions are naturally more conducive for meditative states, you can meditate in any position so long as you are able to relax and focus on your breathing without feeling restricted in any way.

Cleansing techniques

If you want to attain stillness and go into a state of inner peace and awareness, you will find it hard to do this if you are constantly thinking about everyday problems. You have to learn how to let them go for the period of time that you are meditating.

Try this cleansing technique to let go of the everyday worries and stresses before you meditate.

Close your eyes. Focus on your breathing for a moment but don't force it in any way. Wait until you feel your breathing slow down and deepen before you continue.

You are going to create a cleansing sanctuary that is your own personal space. It belongs solely to you and it will be to your own personal design. This is the opportunity for your fertile mind to create something wonderful. You may know it doesn't exist in the real world, but here in the wonderful realm of your imagination anything is possible and you are going to enjoy the creation process.

What do you find most cleansing and comforting? It may be warm water from a bath or shower or fast-flowing, cool water from a stream or river. It could be hot sunlight or perhaps soft, gentle rain. Maybe you just want to imagine pure, brilliant white light streaming down from above as a spiritual or religious cleansing. This is your chance to create what is most powerful for you. Give yourself some time to think about what is most appealing. Choose a scenario that you find both comforting and nurturing.

When you have created an image you like, strengthen your relationship with it by making it as vivid as possible. So if you like the thought of a shower or bath, see it clearly in your mind's eye. Where is it? What size? What colour? Put big, fluffy towels and wonderful smelling soap into this space. Take your time during this process. Savour it.

If you have opted for rich sunlight or gentle rain, where are you when this cleansing takes place? What are your surroundings? Make them as clear as possible. Feel as though you can smell, touch and hear your cleansing space, as well as see it.

If you like the thought of pure white light from above, where is its source? How does that make you feel? Where do you choose to be when this cleansing takes place? Make it as real for you as possible.

WASH AWAY NEGATIVITY

When you feel your cleansing sanctuary is vivid and really powerful as an image for you, then slowly place yourself into it. Stand under that shower, sit in the sunlight, walk in the rain or experience the pure white light. How does it make you feel? You should feel all your worries, fears and problems ebbing or being washed away. This should be a real sensation for you and it should be deeply comforting.

If you can't receive any tangible sensation of cleansing from it, then your cleansing sanctuary is not yet working for you. It should always give a feeling of peace and safety. You should feel calm, renewed and refreshed after time in your cleansing space. Work with this image all the time to make it even richer in imagery, even more powerful in its cleansing ability. You will use it often, so ensure it feels as wonderful as possible.

This cleansing sanctuary is your retreat from negative energy. You can use it at any time before, during and after meditations. It can be used on a daily basis when you want to quickly wash away something unpleasant.

It is always there for you. Look after it well and keep it clean and pure. Never let anyone else into your cleansing sanctuary. It is solely for you. Enjoy it.

Remember to breathe

This is the single most important item on your checklist, because you will accomplish very little if you don't focus on your breath. It is there as a constant reminder for you, because even though you may intend to remember the significance of your breathing at all times, there will still be plenty of occasions when you will forget about it completely.

Most people start off focusing on their breathing and then completely forget about it. You need to return to the power of your breathing throughout the meditation process. Without an awareness of it, you will not be able to move onto a higher level of meditating or get to grips with a particular issue you may have been avoiding or misunderstanding. For many reasons, breathing is always and forever your golden key to meditation.

Relax your muscles

Our bodies carry an enormous amount of physical tension. When we walk, we use about two hundred different muscles. Do you remember to release them when you sit or lie down? Probably not. Try the following exercise to bring about awareness of your muscles and teach you how to relax them.

Sit or lie down and close your eyes. Breathe deeply and let yourself relax. You are going to build a system of awareness around your body, rotating your consciousness, allowing yourself to feel the tension in each part and then learning how to release it.

Start with your right foot. Focus on nothing but this foot. Crunch up your toes and feel the tension seeping through the foot and up your leg. Now take a deep breath in and as you breathe out, relax all the muscles. Enjoy the wonderful sensation of the tension leaving this part of you. Breathe in and out again if you can still feel the tension in the right foot.

Repeat this process, working slowly through your entire body from your foot up your leg to your arms on each side and then from your buttocks up to your back and shoulders, your neck, your head and then down to your chest and stomach.

Remember to focus only on one part of your body at a time. Take a deep breath in as you tense each part and then as you breathe out, feel the tension ebbing away. Then tense the whole body and relax it. Do this several times.

Now, mentally go through your whole body and ask yourself where tension remains. You can do this quite swiftly if you are really focusing. Is your jaw still tight? Release it. Are your shoulders still aching? Release the muscles. Always release on the out breath. Really feel it happen as you exhale.

When you have thoroughly gone through your whole body, lie there quietly for a few minutes, appreciating your newly relaxed, physical body. Notice how much more ready you feel to enter a meditative state. Give yourself a moment to return to reality before you get up and continue your daily life.

Stay hydrated

It is common to find yourself becoming quite dry and thirsty during meditation, particularly as you gradually slip into longer and longer periods of time when you remain still and silent and sink deeper into altered states of consciousness.

As you come out of the meditation and open your eyes, it is a good idea to drink some water, to help rebalance. Often insights come slowly after you have finished; you need some time just to be quiet and digest what you have gleaned. Learn to be gentle with yourself when you finish. Sit for a few minutes silently appreciating what you have learned from your meditation.

Grounding yourself

Sometimes you may find it hard to return to earth after a meditation. You might feel as though your head is still up in the clouds and although it's a lovely feeling, you need to continue with your day. This process of returning to earth is also called grounding yourself.

You know that focusing on your breathing can always help to ground you again, but focusing on your feet is also another effective way of returning to reality after your levels of consciousness have been resting elsewhere. Just ensure that you keep breathing deeply as you do the following grounding exercise.

TRY THIS

* Close your eyes and focus on your feet. (If you choose to meditate lying down, bend your legs so that the soles of your feet are resting flat on the floor. If you are sitting, make sure your legs are not crossed and that your feet are resting flat on the floor.) As you concentrate, realise how heavy your feet feel. They seem to be like lead, solid and secure on the floor. It would be hard for you to lift them.

* Now imagine that the soles of your feet have long roots growing out of them and that these roots are anchored deep into the earth below you. Feel the roots coming out of your feet and going deep into the ground.

* As you focus on your feet, you will slowly feel yourself sinking back into your whole body again. You will become aware that all of you feels comfortably heavy and relaxed. Notice which parts of you are touching the floor, chair or bed and realise how solid they feel.

* Focus on your breathing again as you open your eyes. Become aware of how differently you feel now you are grounded. Wait a moment before you get up.

Part Four
Finding Inner Calm

'Feel a wonderful
golden hue spreading
slowly through every
part of you.'

Going into the stillness

For most of us, our normal state is to be thinking about a number of different issues all at once. This chapter shows you how to find your stillness; a wonderfully quiet, peaceful place that you will go to each and every time you meditate. Try this breathing technique below to help you begin the process.

IN AND OUT MEDITATION

❋ Close your eyes and focus on your breathing. Initially, you just want to observe the breath, nothing more. Settle yourself and give yourself time to focus. If you want to go into your cleansing sanctuary and get rid of anything unwanted, if you want to use your own personal technique to stop other thoughts and emotions from distracting you, that is fine.

❋ Now, as you focus on your breathing you are going to use two simple words to increase your focus. Every time you breathe in, say silently to yourself 'in'. Every time you breathe out, say silently to yourself 'out'. Keep doing this. Say 'in'. Say 'out'. Every time another thought comes into your head, other than these two simple words, acknowledge it but then immediately dismiss it. Let it drift away into nothingness. Nothing exists beyond the words 'in' and 'out'. Keep concentrating for several minutes.

✳ As you do so, notice how your breathing is changing. It is deepening and slowing down. Notice how much slower and how much more of a gap there is between your saying 'in' and 'out'. Take your time as you do this. Keep letting other thoughts drift away. Don't hold on to anything except 'in' and 'out'.

✳ When you are ready, slowly open your eyes and take some time to focus on an object and reorientate yourself. Sip your water and sit quietly for a few minutes.

Playing with numbers

This is another great exercise to help still your mind and improve your concentration.

Close your eyes and focus on your breathing. Acknowledge each breath coming in and going out. Give yourself a few minutes to settle comfortably.

Now when you next breathe in, say 'one'. As you breathe out, say 'one'. Breathe in again and say 'two'. Breathe out and say 'two'. Continue this process. If you get confused and aren't sure which number you are on, return to 'one' and start again. When you successfully get to 'twenty', stop counting.

Now you are going to start again, but this time you want only to think of the number you are currently using. Can you focus solely on the number you are saying, without having your thoughts travel on to the next number or the number you have just said? Can you regard each number as a number and not give it any other significance? This isn't as easy as it sounds! Try it for yourself.

KEEP YOUR FOCUS

The only rule is that you must focus just on the number itself as you breathe in and out; nothing else is allowed to come into your mind. Every time another thought or number comes into your mind, start again at 'one'.

You can vary the way you play with numbers. You can start with any number you like and count downwards. Pick a random number such as '87' and count backwards from it. See how far you can get. Return to the same number and start again when you have to. You can start at another random number and work your way upwards. Choose a high number, such as '999'. Keep focusing on different numbers that will test your ability to concentrate.

THE CANDLE MEDITATION

A simple candle flame can help you work towards discovering the centre of stillness inside you.

* Place a lit candle comfortably in your line of sight, directly in front of you.

* Now close your eyes and spend a moment or two focusing on your breathing. When you feel relaxed and ready, open your eyes and let your focus rest on the candle flame.

* Just gaze gently at the flame. Acknowledge its beauty. Lose yourself in the flame. Let your gaze soften and blur slightly. Feel your awareness melt into the flickering flame itself.

* Focus on nothing but the flame and feel as though you are part of it and it is part of you. You might want to let your eyes close as you do this; you will still see the flickering flame in your mind's eye. If you

feel the flame is starting to fade, open your eyes again and focus on it for a while.

✳ Now allow your awareness of the beauty and warmth of the flame to come into your own body. Imagine this soft, comforting flame coming slowly into the area of your heart. Feel it warm and enrich you.

✳ When you are ready, let yourself feel its glow expanding and filling you. See or sense its wonderful golden hue spreading slowly through every part of you, making you feel warm, relaxed, safe and contented. Enjoy the sensation of peace that comes with it. Everything is all right in your world. Enjoy that knowledge.

✳ After a few minutes, see the flame withdraw from your body, leaving you with the comforting sensation of a wonderful, warm glow inside. Realise the flickering flame is in front of you on top of the candle. Slowly open your eyes and focus on the flame. Give silent thanks for its unique beauty.

FLOWER MEDITATION

✳ Place a beautiful single flower, in water, in front of you. Now close your eyes and relax yourself, using the technique you find most helpful. Work with your breathing and feel it deepen and slow down. When you're ready, open your eyes and focus on the flower head.

✳ Really look at it, without straining, and enjoy its wonderful beauty. Realise how special each flower is and what a work of nature flowers are. Enjoy its texture, its colour. It may even have a scent you can appreciate. Let yourself be filled with wonder and appreciation for this offering from nature.

✳ Let your consciousness melt into the flower itself. Feel what it is like to be a part of nature. Enjoy this comforting sensation. Be aware of what it really means – to be part of the constant ebb and flow of life in all its cycles and seasons.

✳ When you are ready, close your eyes and bring the consciousness of this magnificent flower into your own body. Feel it melt into your physical being and travel into the heart of you. Enjoy its pulsing softness and beauty. Acknowledge how wonderful it makes you feel and the sense of peace which it gives. Wallow in the feeling.

✳ Wait until you feel ready and then let the image of the flower return to the flower in front of you. Withdraw it from your physical body and open your eyes, to see it there in front of you. Give silent thanks for its beauty and to nature, its creator.

✳ Reorientate yourself slowly.

You can, of course, put anything symbolic into this exercise. The simpler the image the more powerful it usually is. Do you have a beautiful seashell that you love? Try meditating on that. A stone, crystal or piece of wood can also be effective.

Going into stillness

This is quite a lengthy exercise that will help you step into the stillness which heralds deeper meditation. Ensure you go through the check list and then settle into your comfortable position. Read through the exercise first, and then when you are ready, begin.

* Close your eyes. Wriggle your body gently into a comfortable position. Start observing your breath. Don't alter it in any way. Notice if you are feeling relaxed or tense. Let yourself go into your cleansing sanctuary for a while. Cleanse and renew your energies. Feel yourself melt into a comfortable state of relaxation.

* Now return to your breathing. Feel each breath coming in and going out. Use whatever technique you wish to lengthen and deepen the breath, such as the stomach, ribcage or balloon breathing exercises. Try the numbers or use the 'in' and 'out' technique. Give yourself time to adjust and let the deeper breathing feel natural and unforced.

* Now you are going to shift your focus from each in and out breath to another area. You are going to feel your focus going to a point deep within your body – the part of you

that is peaceful, still and quiet. You are going to find this area for yourself. It is hidden deep in the middle of your body, below your ribcage and around your navel area. This is the very centre, the very core of you. It is a wonderfully calm, soothing place. You can take your time to find it.

✳ Start by taking your focus from your breathing to the area just below your ribcage. Then let your focus slowly shift from the ribcage to a little further down, towards your belly button. Keep exploring. Take some time to find this area. Give yourself time to find the stillness. There is no rush.

✳ Wait until you can feel the contact. It will probably manifest itself as a slight sensation of something different happening to you. It may be a pleasurable tingle or gentle tickle inside. Perhaps it will feel like a warm glow or a welcome sensation of a cool breeze flowing through you. Everyone feels it differently. Some people even have a scent in their nostrils or a beautiful sound such as tinkling bells in the distance. Give yourself time to find out what your natural reaction is to this new world. Don't rush.

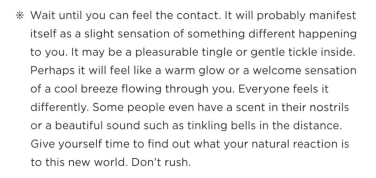

✳ Now let yourself sink into this place. It is so inviting it is easy to do this. Drop slowly into the wonderfully warm, soft enveloping sense of peace. Let yourself really relax into it. Realise how comforted, safe and contented you feel here. Remember to keep your breathing deep and regular. Just let yourself wallow in the pleasure of this new place. Rest here for quite a while. Make a mental note of where this place is within your body and know you will come here again.

COME BACK TO AWARENESS

Then, when you are ready, withdraw your concentration from this area. Let yourself come back to your breathing and focus on each in and out breath. Focus on your real life again. Slowly, bring yourself back to awareness of the present. Notice how heavy your body feels. Slowly open your eyes and focus on an object. Sip your water and wait a while before you get up.

How did your physical body feel after that experience? You may have felt strange when you first opened your eyes. You may have felt you didn't really find this stillness. You may just have felt relaxed, or maybe you know you didn't find what you were supposed to. Whatever your experience, that is fine.

THE RETREAT MEDITATION

While some techniques work inward into silence, this beautiful meditation starts with an awareness of outer influences.

* Start off by settling yourself comfortably in your meditating position. Close your eyes, and relax into your deeper breathing.

* Now you want to take your awareness to outside sounds. Really listen to see what you can hear outside. Can you hear a plane flying? Perhaps birds are twittering in the trees. Perhaps you can hear people walking down the street, chatting. Whatever you hear, try to identify it and then let it fade from your consciousness. Make sure you have fully identified all the distant sounds you can hear.

* Now move a little closer in to your own surroundings. What can you hear just outside the room you are in? Is there the hum of electrical appliances? Are floorboards creaking or is there a whirr of heating or air conditioning? Maybe you can hear a pet moving around the house or even snoring. Really listen to the sounds outside your room. As soon as you recognise them, let them float away.

✳ Now bring your focus to the room you are presently in. What sounds can you hear in the room itself? Is there the ticking of a clock? Perhaps a breeze is blowing through the window. Again, listen intently to anything you can identify within the room itself but try not to hold on to the awareness of the sound. Let it fade away.

✳ Now start to bring your awareness closer in to you, just around your body itself. Become aware of the space your physical body occupies and tune in to that. What can you hear? What is that new sound you now hear? Focus. If you listen closely enough you will hear it. It is a gentle, repetitious thudding sound, faint but persistent. Can you hear it?

✳ It is your heartbeat. Listen to it. Enjoy it. This is your very life source, work your body does day in, day out, to keep you alive and healthy. Appreciate the sound. Really become aware of it. Move your awareness within your own body to access its centre. Take a journey into your heart area and appreciate the strength and beauty residing there.

✳ As you move inside, be aware of other sounds within your body. Can you hear your stomach gurgling as its digests? Can you feel your veins pulsing gently in other parts of your body? Realise what a powerhouse of activity takes place constantly in your own body. Give silent thanks for its divine existence.

THE SOUND OF SILENCE

Now move deeper into the very core of your body. Can you find an area that is deep, dark, silent and still? Gently explore with your conscious thought. As you do so, let the other sounds in your body fade into the distance. Become aware gradually that there are no more sounds. No sounds remain. Only silence. There is only wonderful silence – pure, clear silence that is infinitely comforting and peaceful. Nothing exists here but stillness and a wonderful sense of nothingness. Rest in this absolute silence and stillness for as long as you like. If any thoughts come into your head, let them fade away. Enjoy the sensation of nothingness. Savour it.

Then, very slowly, bring your awareness back to the everyday sounds around you. Realise that the clock is ticking. You can hear the wind in the trees or the rain on the window. Really focus on everyday sounds again. Gently, open your eyes and focus on the room you are in. Sip your water. Take your time to return to present day.

Part Five
Sounds and Scents

'The power of a mantra
lies in your ability to
lose yourself in its rich,
sonorous sound.'

Discovering mantras

The sounds we can make ourselves have long been used in meditating. Making a sound and repeating it constantly is known as a 'mantra'. Most ancient forms of meditation use mantras, as indeed do many of the more modern, Western forms of meditation, which regard them as the main method through which inner calm can be discovered.

Because making a strange noise and continuously repeating it might feel odd to you, it is doubly important for this type of meditation that you are in a quiet place, and will not be disturbed. You might also want to ensure that no one else is within earshot.

First, choose a sound and then, breathing deeply and comfortably, utter that sound out loud, slowly and sonorously. The sound will last as long as your breath. Stop only to refill your lungs and then continue. Does this feel rather strange to you? Perhaps you are wondering how this can possibly be a powerful experience.

HUM A TUNE

Now try something else. Take a comfortable, deep breath and then hum a low note quietly to yourself. Pitch the note near the bottom of your register so that it resonates inside you. How does that feel in your body? Can you feel a sort of tingle or vibration deep inside? Take another deep breath and quietly hum a high note near the top of your register. How different is that as a sensation within your body? Did you notice different parts of your body react to each note? Did you find the high note or the low note more comfortable?

For meditative purposes, it is accepted that a lower note is more in harmony with your body and that it is easier to relax with a lower note than a high, piercing one. So, apart from choosing your lower register, what else do you need to create an effective mantra?

SIMPLE SOUNDS

First, it's better not to use a real word. Although some words, such as 'peace' or 'calm', might sound very comforting, the problem is that you may be tempted to think about their meaning and what the words mean to you. The purpose and power of a mantra lies in your ability to lose yourself in its rich, sonorous sound and the way it vibrates around and through your body. If you are thinking consciously or unconsciously about the word, it stops the mantra from doing its job.

A mantra should be no more than one or two syllables. It is the simplicity of the sound that will help you to focus.

You want something you can repeat continuously without effort and conscious thought.

Certain consonants are more helpful than others for meditating. Let's do another experiment to help prove this. Quietly utter the 's' sound to yourself. Now say the 'n' sound softly to yourself. Which feels richer and vibrates more? Try saying the 't' sound. Now say the 'w' sound. You'll probably agree that the 'n' and 'w' sounds vibrate through you. The 't' and 's' sounds seem sharper, higher and less resonant.

So, you want to find a word that has no recognisable meaning, that has only one or two syllables and that consists of consonants which resonate in a rich, comforting way in and around your body. Creating a mantra is a very personal matter, so it is good if you can discover your own word for yourself.

Suggested mantras

You may want to choose one of the following or use one of them as a guideline. You may want to put two of the syllables together.

MAH - NUM	SOHM	DA - YAM
VO - HUM	WONE	RAH - MAH
RAHM	VEE - NONG	SHAH - LOON
LAH - NEE	PRAH	

There are many others you can create. Choose another sound altogether if it feels right for you. The only way to know which sound works for you is to try them all or create your own while in a relaxed state. When you are ready, work through the following exercise.

THE MANTRA MEDITATION

✳ Choose the word you will concentrate on and then close your eyes. Use your cleansing and breathing techniques and allow yourself to sink into a comfortably relaxed state.

✳ Now see your word in your mind's eye. How does it look to you? How does the word make you feel? Take a deep breath and speak it slowly and sonorously to yourself. It can be spoken quite softly if you like. Let the word continue until you have finished the breath. If there are two syllables, try to balance them out equally in your breath although you may find this difficult at first. Just keep making the sound until your breath runs out. Then take a deep breath in and repeat the process. Do this at least three times with the word.

✳ Notice what feelings and sensations come to you at this time. Where do you feel the vibrations in your body?

✳ Really feel the word vibrate through and around you. Lose yourself in the word, completely. Feel it spread outwards from you in a wonderful glow of energy. Let yourself merge with the sound and then become nothing but the sound itself. You will find that you are unaware when you are breathing in because the sound seems continuous as its vibrations spread ever wider and intensify. Stay in this state for some time.

DISCOVER YOUR WORD

When you are ready, slowly prepare to withdraw from your word. To do this, start chanting the word more slowly and more quietly. Gradually, make it softer and softer. Let it gently fade into nothingness. If this has been powerful for you, then you may find it is quite difficult to let the vibrations of the sound disappear. Give yourself some time for this to happen. Cleanse it away if you need to. Don't rush the process.

Let yourself sit in the stillness for a while. Enjoy the silence. Now you might want to discover if there is a mantra out there for you which is personal and right for you. Focus on this possibility. Ask for help. Say you would like to be given your own private mantra that will work powerfully for you. See if anything comes to you. Sit quietly and wait with your eyes closed. Keep concentrating on the possibility of there being a word that is meant just for you and that will be revealed in your state of higher awareness.

When you open your eyes, you may find that the room suddenly feels very bright and clear. It may seem as though it is pulsating with light. You may notice you are tingling with a vibrant energy you haven't felt before. Ensure you give yourself plenty of time to readjust again. Sip your water very slowly. Sit quietly for five minutes before you get up.

Using other sounds

There are also other sounds you might choose to have around you while you meditate. It does not have to be you making the sound; it can be an external force. You might prefer to focus on your breathing and let other sounds wash over you without your having actually to make them.

So, if you choose an outside sound, what might you enjoy and find soothing? This is, of course, very personal and you will have to experiment and see what works best for you.

Now is your chance to learn about what sounds you find therapeutic. Let's start with certain sounds of nature. Do you like the sound of the wind rustling the leaves of trees? Perhaps waves pounding on a seashore or the rush of a powerful waterfall make you feel good. Bird song can be wonderfully uplifting and relaxing.

SHAKE IT UP

There are plenty of man-made sounds as well. What about drums beating or rattles shaking? These are used in many Indian and Shamanic practices. The ringing of bells is used by Buddhists to bring about awareness. You might prefer the sound of flutes or harps.

During your meditations try experimenting with different types of sounds and see what works. Buy a small wind chime and place it in a breeze by a window. See what that feels like to you. You can even get a

glass jar, fill it with dried beans and shake it. What does that sound feel like to you? If you like it, why don't you record it onto your phone and play it back.

You may be surprised that certain noises really are helpful and comforting. Let yourself enjoy the learning process of sound and its effects and take your time. There is always some new sound for you to experiment with.

The power of scent

Appreciation of scents has existed since early man. Aromatherapy, the art of using essential oils to nurture and balance our energy system, is one of the most ancient forms of healing, while flowers and incense can also be incredibly beneficial.

So what scents are going to be helpful for you? Now is the time for you to start experimenting.

Certain flowers have very powerful odours; which ones do you like? Make a habit of sniffing the flowers you come across. This is another wonderful way of living your life in daily awareness. When you stop and smell a flower, it's impossible not to be filled with appreciation for its beauty.

If the area in which you live is very barren flower-wise, then notice what trees you have around you and, when they come into flower, stop and smell their flowers. You can also go into florist shops or stop and study the flowers sold on stalls. Certain flowers, such as freesias and lilies, have very strong aromas which can literally fill a small room with a glorious scent. Do you like the sweet perfume of lilies? Perhaps you prefer the delicate scent of roses.

When you next take a walk in a park or forest, stop and smell the plants. Certain house plants – scented geraniums, for example – can make wonderful additions to your meditation room. Simply brush your hand delicately across a geranium and the scent will linger on your skin. Give yourself time to experience this new appreciation of the world of scent.

Flowers and plants

Certain flowers are said to have specific purposes and produce particular effects. This does not mean that you will necessarily respond in the way suggested to all of them, but it might be useful for you to try some of the scents listed below and note your reactions to them.

TRY THESE

❊ **Apple blossom:** divination; health and romance

❊ **Carnation:** self love; physical passion

❊ **Garlic:** protection; health

❊ **Scented geranium:** affirming appreciation of life

❊ **Goldenrod:** protection

❊ **Honeysuckle:** youth

❊ **Hyacinth:** gentleness; femininity

❊ **Jasmine:** self-esteem; psychic development; dreamwork

❊ **Lavender:** inner guidance; spiritual contact

❊ **Lilac:** travel; past lives

❊ **Lily:** spiritual love; purity

❊ **Rose:** awareness of the heart and love; beauty

Essential oils

These precious oils are also a wonderful way to enhance your appreciation of smell when you meditate. Put a few drops in an incense burner or in your bath water and make a note of how you react to different aromas. Really observe how your meditations differ when you try different oils as all of them have different properties. Do some make you want to meditate on different areas of your life? Is there a specific feeling that always comes over you when you use a particular oil?

There are also certain oils you would want to avoid in special circumstances, such as pregnancy. If in doubt, always consult with the shop before purchasing. Never put pure essential oils directly onto your skin; they are too powerful and can cause skin irritation, and make sure you buy quality oils which only contain the pure essence.

TRY THESE

❋ **Cedarwood:** enhances connection to spirit

❋ **Chamomile:** for inner peace

❋ **Clary sage:** balances mind and emotions

❋ **Eucalyptus:** clears negativity

❋ **Lemon:** increases energy and encourages clarity

❋ **Marjoram:** calms agitated mind

❋ **Neroli:** opens heart and enhances creativity

❋ **Rosemary:** helps increase spiritual awareness

❋ **Rosewood:** enhances meditation

❋ **Vetiver:** aids stillness (known as the 'oil of tranquillity')

Keep a scent and smell diary

When you have exhausted all the flowers, plants and essences around you, turn your attention to different kinds of incense. Fortunately, many shops nowadays sell individual incense sticks, giving you the opportunity to try a variety of scents without incurring great cost. Buy just one or two and burn them in your room as you meditate. Notice what happens and which scents you react favourably to and which make you feel uncomfortable. You might find it useful to keep a scent diary, to monitor your reaction to these new odours.

If you find that you are responding positively to different scents, you might consider investing a little more and to work with more advanced concoctions. A good health or new age shop will be able to provide you with incense sticks that have been specially prepared with natural odours known to enhance meditation.

Notice what happens and which scents you react favourably to and which make you feel uncomfortable.

TRY DIFFERENT COMBOS

As you continue with your meditations, also continue developing your relationship with sounds and smells, as this will increase your ability to sink into your newly discovered world of stillness and peace. Really work at finding your perfect combinations. You might find it useful to keep a scent and smell diary, to monitor your reaction to these new combinations.

Perhaps it is bird song in the background with vetiver essence around you. Maybe you prefer harp music and the smell of lilies in your nostrils.

Keep being aware on a daily basis of what is really happening to you and allow yourself to use sound and smells as a helpful balancing tool. Continue using these new tools of awareness as complements to all the new techniques you are about to explore.

What's in a word?

Focusing on a simple word once we are in our meditative state can help our thoughts reach new levels. You will already have seen how a word in the form of a mantra might help you. Now we are going to look at known words and see how awareness of something we recognise can take on a greater level of significance when we are meditating.

Do you often feel that you don't understand the true significance of words, that they elude you in a maddeningly abstract way? This can be true of even relatively simple words you think you ought to know, such as 'peace' or 'stillness'. We are going to continue using words as a wonderful means of showing you what else you can learn about yourself and others. Spend a little time meditating on some of the words listed below and see what each one tells you about aspects of life.

WORDS FOR MEDITATION

Peace	Power	Infinity
Stillness	Conscience	Fate
Cosmos	Life	Time
Truth	Universe	Duality
Honesty	Purpose	Knowledge
Happiness	Destiny	Love
Money	Meditation	

No doubt you can think of words of your own and add them to the list. Do make sure that when you meditate, you take yourself fully into that state of stillness before you continue. You might like to write your chosen word in large letters on a piece of paper and prop it up in front of you. Whenever you feel lost or stuck, you can then open your eyes and look at the word for fresh inspiration.

WORD MEDITATION

During these meditations you might find it helpful to keep a word diary as some of what we meditate upon can be lost to our conscious memory shortly after we finish meditating.

✳ Close your eyes and settle yourself comfortably. Relax, breathe deeply and let yourself enter your inner stillness. Rest there for a moment and then, when you are ready, open your eyes and look at your chosen word.

✳ What is the first thought that comes into your head? Ask yourself why this is your response. See if a personal experience has triggered this reaction. Then let the feeling drift away. Say the word out loud or say it silently to yourself. Do certain images or sensations come with it? Let yourself flow with those reactions, but try not to become deeply involved with any of them. If you have feelings you don't want, remember to keep washing them away.

✳ Let yourself play with the word. Have it dance it front of you. Have it become bold print or capitals or a beautifully flowing scroll. Bounce the word up and down like a ball. Sniff it. Eat it! You are free to respond however you wish. No one will know.

✳ Now make the word become more personal to you. Where does this word manifest itself in your life? Where might you like it to be? What would you have to do to make this happen?

✳ When you are ready, withdraw from the word. If it has really come alive for you during the meditation, you may find it difficult to let the word go. Use your cleansing techniques to get rid of it. Burn it, wash it away, have it float upwards in a balloon – whatever is powerful for you. Cleanse yourself again before you open your eyes.

Everyday meditations

The technique of using a single word to let your mind spiral onto other levels can also work in improving your toleration of mundane jobs. Are you struggling with the daily washing or a work task or the routine of collecting the children from school each day? Whatever you want to give extra meaning to, simply meditate on the action.

At this stage, it is probably easier if you use one word or two to identify the action, such as 'collecting children' or 'washing'. If you try to complicate it with long sentences you are going to be throwing a lot of emotions into the meditation and any insights you receive may be confused and jumbled as a result. To create powerful and helpful meditations, you need to make the concept you are meditating on as simple as possible.

If you are meditating on a personal subject, and are struggling with it, for whatever reason, remember that you will have to keep putting aside your own negative feelings during the meditation. If it is an emotional issue for you, then it is natural that your own emotions will be uppermost as you start. This is where the cleansing techniques become so valuable.

TRUE WISDOM

You will soon discover that it is your own preconceived thoughts about how everything ought to be which get in the way of you moving past the ordinary and progressing into the layers of deep subconscious thought, which is where our true wisdom and knowledge lies. Meditation teaches us just how human we are, and how our individual traits can sometimes stop us from achieving greater awareness.

We have to embrace our human behaviour before we can move past it to the higher levels. That is why you are constantly being reminded about awareness of everyday matters and how to bring this into your meditations. By truly embracing our very human responses to everything, we can learn how to let go of them during meditation and understand life on a much deeper level.

Do spend time assessing your everyday life through meditation. See what insights come to you through meditating on very simple words such as those below: There are probably quite a few of your own words that you want to add to this list, so feel free to do so!

DAILY WORDS

Washing	Marriage	Mortgage
Cleaning	Partner	Rent
Ironing	Child	Home
Cooking	Parent	Garden
Career	Sibling	Carer

Let yourself enjoy the experience of meditating with each word and notice what insights come to you. Do you find you are developing the ability to view areas of your life in a different way? Of course, some areas you will always find more challenging and frustrating than others. When these crop up, don't worry. If nothing really helpful or insightful happens in an area which you desperately want to understand more, let the emotions wash away and know that shortly you are going to learn some more techniques to help you deal with the heavier issues.

Using visual images

In this section, we're going to be looking at different visual images and assessing what impact they have on you. We are talking about physical images now, not the sort you create in your imagination, although, as you will discover, one can directly affect the other.

Just as you have been discovering what you truly feel about different sounds and smells, now is the opportunity for you to find out what visual images you find helpful and enlightening.

CHOOSING AN IMAGE

First, you are going to consider what visual images help you to relax into a meditative state. After that, we will look at different, more complex images that may help you once you are in a meditative state.

We will begin by thinking about what images you find relaxing. Just as with mantras, you don't want to find yourself getting too caught up with the meaning of the image. If there are people in your image, chances are you will start thinking about what is happening to those people in the image. The simpler and more appealing the image is, the better. A small crystal, a vase of flowers, a picture of the sea, a photo of the moon, a postcard of a tree or other objects of nature.

Relaxing images can also be found in the surface of items that you might well have around you already. Have you noticed how beautiful the grain in wood can be? The same is true of a piece of driftwood, a stone or crystal. A seashell is also an object of enormous intricacy and appeal. Look at a single leaf on a plant. Even the skin on a piece of fruit can be beautiful.

In your daily mindfulness of everything, take time to appreciate what is around you.

Choose your colours

R elaxation in terms of visual images is heavily linked to colour; most people find pastel shades much more relaxing than sharp, bright colours. Do the images that soothe you most have colours that are muted and harmonious together? The colour green is known to encourage growth, harmony and loving thoughts; blue is found to have a very cooling and calming effect.

Soft pink is also known to have a calming effect while soft warm purples are considered beneficial for enhancing spiritual awareness. Are you drawn to any of these colours?

If you have only chosen bright reds and fiery oranges so far, carefully consider whether they will properly soothe you for meditation. This is not to say that you are wrong for choosing them; you might have found the picture of a setting sun painted in rich reds and oranges to be the most inspirational image for you.

VISUAL MEDITATION

✳ When you have chosen your image, start by relaxing and concentrating on your breathing. You might want to close your eyes while you do this. You don't have to wait until you enter into your inner stillness because you are going to let the visual image do this for you; just ensure you are relaxed and comfortable first.

✳ Now open your eyes and let your gaze rest on the image or object you have chosen. Don't stare at it; let your gaze be soft and slightly hazy. If you find thoughts coming into your head, keep washing them away. You don't need them now. Empty yourself of responses to what is in front of you. Just let it rest there without judgement or meaning. This is all you have to do. Simply enjoy its beauty.

✳ As you keep your eyes focused on the image or object, notice that it seems to be coming nearer. It may feel as though it is becoming part of you or that you are approaching it and merging; it doesn't matter which.

✳ Let your consciousness slip slowly into the image. Feel yourself slide down into the swirls of the wood, or the petals of the flower or the intricate design of the shell or beauty of the object in front of you. This may be a gradual process and may take a long time, or you may feel yourself swept away on a wonderful wave of awareness. Whatever happens for you, it is right.

YOUR MIND'S EYE

As this happens, you may find your eyes closing. You will find yourself sinking comfortably into your familiar world of peace and quiet, your private inner core. Let yourself slide quickly and easily into this state. You may notice that your image or object has come with you and is still visible in your mind's eye.

Ask silently why it has come with you into your inner world of silence and retreat. See what it is you are meant to learn from its presence. Spend some time together and enjoy its comforting presence. Let any pictures or sensations come and go in waves of awareness. Don't try to hold onto anything. Rest there for as long as it feels right for you.

Then slowly withdraw. Come back to your everyday world gradually, releasing the image or object from your mind's eye as you do so. Use your cleansing methods to get rid of everything you don't want. Wait until you are properly grounded again before you continue.

Part Six
Working with Energy

'Everything we say and do
gives off a subtle energy.'

Your aura

You know something about your physical body and what it can do, but have you ever thought of yourself as being more than purely physical? In your early stages of meditation, you will no doubt have discovered that this quiet inner core you find inside yourself doesn't actually seem to be a tangible area, but more a feeling or sensation which comes over you.

Have you sometimes entered a space and been struck by how pleasant it feels without any obvious reasons for it? Likewise, you can also go into a room and suddenly feel very uneasy, without any obvious physical indication as to why you feel this way. Just as with people, you are immediately drawn to some rooms and you feel you want to return to them, to enjoy the feeling of that space.

FEEL THE POWER

So what are you tapping into when you have these responses? The simple answer is: energy! Everything we say and do gives off a subtle energy, or what we call an aura. If the emotion is very strong, we can actually pick up on it and want to react to it. Think about this in terms of what you sense from other people. Do some people give off comforting energy and others make you immediately feel uncomfortable? When someone is in love, can you sense or almost see a golden glow of pleasure around them? Think about the effect of being around someone who is permanently 'on edge' and distraught. Now think of being in the calming influence of a gentle and wise figure who is always smiling. Would you say that you can almost tangibly feel these energies, even though they aren't visible to you in a physical sense?

TUNING IN TO MEDITATION

By learning how to tap into your own and other people's energy you can learn to understand who you really are. You will need to find a willing and enthusiastic friend to help you explore the energies people give out.

* Sit opposite each other, just a few feet apart, and close your eyes. Both of you need to take a moment to focus yourselves and to breathe deeply. Both of you should keep your eyes closed throughout.

* Now one of you chooses to be the Giver and the other the Receiver. The Giver concentrates on a particular emotion while the Receiver sits quietly and relaxes. The Giver needs time to let the emotion become real and vivid to them. However, the Giver at no time speaks or articulates the emotion, they simply feel it and let it seep out of them in an energetic form towards the Receiver. Ensure you work with strong emotions such as anger, peacefulness, joy, sadness.

✳ When the Receiver is ready, they
then tune in to what is coming at
them. Remembering to keep their eyes
closed, they simply focus on what they feel
coming at them in waves from the Giver. They
then check with the Giver if their feelings are
accurate. Both of you then need to cleanse the
emotion away before you continue.

✳ Have another try or swap over so that the Giver
becomes the Receiver and vice versa. You may find one
person is more sensitive to picking up energy than the
other. The only rule is that you must always remember to
cleanse afterwards and ensure that the last emotion you
choose is a positive one that leaves you both feeling good.

AURA MEDITATION

N ot all people see auras, although you can train yourself to do so. Try the experiment below one day when you have some uninterrupted time.

✳ Arrange a full-length mirror in front of you and a plain, white light behind you. Make sure the area behind you is as dark and plain as possible. It is hard to see auras against patterned backgrounds.

✳ Now sit or stand quietly in front of the mirror for a few moments. Focus on your breathing and look inwardly for a

while, ignoring your own reflection. You might want to close
your eyes for this, although if you are standing you might
find this makes you feel unbalanced. Calm and still yourself.

✳ When you are ready, open your eyes and focus on the
area just around your head. Let your gaze soften, don't
stare too hard. Can you see anything? Remember to keep
breathing and don't try too hard. Can you see a vague
light? Perhaps it is like a fuzzy white haze or a golden glow.
It may encompass the whole head or only seem to be there
in sections. It may seem like the light that a candle flame
gives off. You may see nothing at all. Concentrate on the
area around your head for a while.

✳ Then let your focus be drawn to other areas around your
body. Can you see anything near your heart area? (Like
the head, this is another part that can give off and receive
powerful energy.) Let your focus shift to different areas of
your body and notice when you can see anything. Don't
worry if you can see very little.

✳ When you have finished, remember to wash away anything
you didn't like. Take a moment to ground yourself when you
have finished.

HAND ENERGY MEDITATION

You might also find it helpful to feel your own aura. Your aura is around all of you at all times; you can't get away from it or separate it in any way from you, so it is always there to work with or play with. A good way to become aware of your energy is to use your hands. Try the next exercise.

✳ Take some deep breaths and relax. Take your time. Now hold your hands up in front of you, palms facing each other, but about eighteen inches apart. Have your fingers straight but close together rather than spread open. Now slowly, very, very slowly, move your hands in towards each other. Really take your time over this, do it gradually and with complete awareness.

✳ Before you get very far, you will feel a slight pulling sensation, as if there is something happening between your two hands. You may want to move your hands apart a little. Now move them in again. What can you feel? Slowly, very slowly, move your hands closer and closer together. At some point, you may actually feel as though you can't move them any closer together; it may feel as though a force is keeping them apart. This is your own energy, your own aura.

✳ Play with your aura, feel it bounce back and forth between your hands. Try to pat it into a round ball. Let it stretch outwards until you can't feel it and then move it in again. When you have finished, give your hands a good shake and release any restricted energy.

Could you feel that quite strongly? It's a good way to acknowledge there is some interaction of energy taking place, although you can't actually see it. If you do this exercise again sometime, you may actually be able to see some light playing back and forth between your hands.

The layers of the aura

The human aura is known to contain at least seven separate layers of energy, each one becoming finer and lighter in intensity as it radiates outwards from the body.

Below is an outline of each of the seven layers of the aura. The first layer is closest to the physical body and is the part that most people see initially when they start focusing on auras. The others radiate outwards sequentially.

First layer

The physical self; about being earthed and grounded, enjoying all physical activities and pursuits and everything to do with 'earthly' living.

Second layer

The emotional self in relation to one's life; about self-expression and self-love.

Third layer

The mental self; to do with rational thoughts and our ability to rationalise.

Fourth layer

Conditional love; how we feel about others and how we relate to them. Here the energies start to become lighter and finer and harder to see.

Fifth layer

Divine will, the releasing of personal ambitions and emotions; about our ability to see life as part of a larger picture and to understand where we fit in.

Sixth layer

Divine love; unconditional and all-encompassing love, allowing us to understand everything in the larger context of universal laws, rather than through earthly attachments.

Seventh layer

Divine mind; about fusing with all spiritual awareness and becoming one with universal truths and laws. Described as a state of bliss.

The chakras

To work on your aura, you first have to discover the door into these layers of energy. These doors are called chakras, the ancient Sanskrit word for 'wheel' and their existence has been known for thousands of years.

The seven chakras are basically the entrance into the human aura. They are located at specific parts of the human body. Our body is a very complex criss-cross of energy lines; it is believed that there are more than seventy-two thousand separate lines of energy running through the human body at all angles. Each of the seven chakras, which are often likened to the multiple petals of a lotus flower, is located at a point where twenty-one lines of energy cross the body.

It is through our increased awareness of the chakras that we can gain access into our auras, and thereby understand a great deal more about the purpose of our life on every level.

You may not have realised it at the time, but when you were meditating on different areas in your life and different issues that have affected you, you were unconsciously tapping into some of these chakras and working with them.

Below is a run-down of each chakra and its significance. You will notice that each chakra relates to each layer of the aura.

Base chakra

Located at the base of the spine and opens downwards to the ground. Its associated colour is red and physically it is related to the spinal column, the adrenal glands and the kidneys. This chakra is about your physical sense of being and your appreciation of earthly life, such as love of food, sexual relations and all physical activities. It is often called the 'root' of you, because it shows how rooted you are in all earthly matters. It is also about your instinct for survival, your 'flight or fight' metabolism.

Navel chakra

This is found just below the navel and opens front and back through the body. Sometimes it is known as the sacral chakra. It is associated with the colour orange and is connected to the reproductive system and our immune system. This is about our sexuality, but not simply referring to the sexual act itself. It deals with how well you form relationships with others, whether sexual or not. It is about your emotions in relation to this. Given that sexuality is a difficult area for many people, this chakra needs special sensitivity and gentleness.

Solar plexus chakra

This is situated just below the breastbone, slightly to the left. It opens both front and back. The colour given is yellow. It is affiliated to the pancreas gland and the stomach, gall bladder, liver and nervous system. This is where you store your mental perception of yourself; it is about self-esteem and how you see yourself fitting into life. It is the seat of your will-power and reflects how you digest information.

Heart chakra

This is found in the middle of the breast-bone and above the chest, and opens both front and back. It is connected to the colour green and associated with the thymus gland, the heart, blood and the circulatory system. This is about love; not just your ability to love yourself and others, but also how you love the universe as a whole. The subtle energies start to change here and become lighter and finer. The heart chakra is often considered the hinge or link between the physical and spiritual worlds: the point at which true spiritual awareness can start to develop.

Throat chakra

This is located at the hollow of the throat and has two openings, front and back. The colour sky blue is connected to this chakra, which relates to the thyroid gland, bronchial tubes and vocal organs, lungs and alimentary canal. This is about how we hear inner truths and learn how to speak them.

It reflects what we feel about our professional life, too, and how we can expand our awareness on every level. This is about integrity of speech and living through higher awareness.

Brow chakra

Situated in the middle of the forehead, this opens both front and back. Purple is the related colour and it's connected to the pituitary gland, lower brain, left eye, ears, nose and nervous system. This is often called our 'third eye' and is about our vision to see, not in a literal sense but in a much wider, truly spiritual and universal context. As the energies become yet finer and higher, so these concepts become harder to grasp without literally experiencing them.

Crown chakra

This is found at the very top and centre of the head. It has only one opening, upwards to the sky. It is associated with the colour violet, although it is sometimes also referred to as white, since the crown chakra symbolises true purity at all levels of consciousness. The body parts it is connected to are the pineal gland, upper brain and right eye. As this is the highest and finest of all the subtle energies, it is the most difficult to explain. It is related to a state of pure bliss, a sense of understanding and awareness that transcends all earthly words. It is supreme connection and merging with the divine. It is a state to which one can aspire, without necessarily understanding all it encompasses.

Opening your chakras

To consciously open all your chakras and to enjoy the new sensation that comes from this heightened awareness make sure you follow the usual guidelines. Alternate nostril breathing is strongly recommended too.

Settle yourself comfortably and close your eyes. Remember to take your time to breathe deeply and relax.

START AT THE BOTTOM OF YOUR SPINE

This is your base chakra. Simply bring your focus to this part of your body. Remember this chakra only opens downwards to the ground and it is never closed. What can you feel? Perhaps you may feel a little heaviness in the area or a pulsing of light or energy. Think of the colour red if you like, to help you focus. Now feel how it is moving. Wait until you have acknowledged this chakra before you move on.

MOVE UP TO YOUR BELLY BUTTON

Just below you'll find your navel chakra, which has two openings, front and back, so make sure you focus on both. Can you feel a little tickle as the chakra starts to open? Perhaps it is open already. Can you speed up its vibrations by encouraging it to move a little faster? Focus on the colour orange.

UP TO YOUR BREAST BONE

Slightly to the left you'll find your solar plexus chakra. Use the focus of the colour yellow to help you. Remember, this chakra opens both front and back. Give yourself time to feel it opening. Every chakra feels different, so don't worry if there is no repeated sensation when you concentrate on each chakra in turn. Just let yourself feel whatever is happening without judging.

ON TO YOUR HEART

Your heart chakra is where the energies start to change and become finer and brighter. Focus on your heart area and remember this chakra opens front and back. Try to balance the flow between the two. Let the colour green come into your conscious thought and feel it flowing through the heart chakra.

THE HOLLOW OF YOUR THROAT

Concentrate here on the throat chakra. Feel it opening front and back. Notice if the feeling makes you want to swallow or clear your throat? Focus on the colour blue of a clear sky.

MOVE UP TO YOUR FOREHEAD

The spot in the middle is the brow chakra. Feel it opening front and back. Bring the colour purple into this area and see how that affects the chakra opening. The brow chakra is called the 'third eye' by clairvoyants, who focus on it to attain higher energies.

THE CROWN CHAKRA

Finally move to the top and middle of your head. This has only one opening, upwards to the sky. It is always open, but you want to feel it open a little more. Focus on it and notice what you feel. The crown chakra seems to be powerful on physical as well as etheric levels.

CLEANSE YOUR AURA

Finally let yourself slip into your cleansing sanctuary and cleanse your whole aura by letting the water or light come down through each chakra, starting with the crown, and very gently washing away anything you don't want. Take this process very slowly, and enjoy it. Carefully go through each chakra in reverse: crown, brow, throat, heart, solar plexus, navel and base. Enjoy the sensation of all your energies feeling more alive and receptive to everything around you, both physically and spiritually.

CLOSING YOUR CHAKRAS MEDITATION

Opening up can be a wonderful sensation but it's essential that you also learn how to close down properly, so you are properly grounded before you continue in the everyday world.

* Cleanse by using your usual technique. Feel anything you don't want being washed away with your light or water. You want to ensure nothing unpleasant remains in your energy field before you close your chakras.

* Now, starting with the base chakra, feel the chakra gently slowing down under your focus. Remember this chakra always stays open to a certain extent, but it will have become much more active during your concentration. Feel it gradually slow down. You will still sense it pulsing or moving slightly but know it is now moving in a gentle, less energetic way.

* Move up to the navel chakra. Concentrate on this area and feel the chakra slowly close, both front and back. It is useful to create your own image for this, to make the action more powerful. Imagine the petals of a flower folding up or a door closing or whatever you find works best for you.

* Continue this process up through the solar plexus, heart, throat and brow, remembering to close each chakra both front and back. When you reach the crown, remember that this chakra stays open at all times but you want to slow down its energies. Feel it pulsing at a lower rate or shining less brightly.

Sometimes after closing your chakras, you can still feel slightly light-headed from your new state of awareness. Remember to use your grounding energy exercise and focus on your feet. Notice how heavy your body feels in the chair. Always use this as a grounding tool before you get up again when you are working consciously with your chakras.

CLOAK OF PROTECTION MEDITATION

This effective technique will help you feel more secure after a sensitive meditation. You can use it at any time, whether finishing a meditation or stuck in a crowded bus or train or feeling bombarded by someone else's energies.

You are going to create your own invisible cloak of protection that you can call upon at any time to wrap around you.

* Sit quietly and close your eyes. Breathe deeply. Let yourself settle and become still. Slip into the state of inner silence that you love and are beginning to know well. Sit quietly for a few minutes.

* Now, silently ask that you be given your own personal cloak of protection. Wait for a little while. Don't expect instant results. Gradually, something will be shown to you. You will see it, feel it or sense it. It is your own personal cloak of protection, so it will be something that is right and powerful for you. It may come in the shape of brilliant light that surrounds you and gives you a feeling of safety. You may be given shimmering armour or a fabric that is waterproof and warm.

FEEL SAFE

Whatever you put on, it should immediately make you feel good. You shouldn't feel heavy, restricted or claustrophobic. It may not have any earthly connection so it may be a sensation rather than a physical image for you. All that is required is that it makes you feel safe and insulated from any unwanted outside influences. This cloak of protection does not shut you off from everyone. You can still give out your energies and receive back what you want to receive. But nothing unwanted can bombard you. Nothing unpleasant can get through.

The cloak of protection is yours forever. Call up on it any time you need it and release it any time you don't.

Part Seven

Free Your Mind

'Breathe into the silence
and embrace the sacred
stillness.'

Freeing meditations

The meditations you will experience in this chapter are designed to free your mind and enable you to relax.

You can experience these meditations in the same way as you have the others: by reading each one through first, then closing your eyes and running through them in your mind, remembering as much as you can. However, consider trying something different. Why not record yourself or the voice of a friend reciting the meditation?

It is important to choose someone whose voice you really enjoy listening to, not someone whose accent or energy you find difficult or distracting. Your relaxation will come from the content of the meditation and the timbre of the voice of the person who is speaking. The voice should be calm but not monotone, steady without being too slow, and warm without being syrupy.

REMEMBER THE GUIDELINES

Although these are freeing meditations, you still want to take into account all the requirements on your meditation checklist. If you want to test the theory, you might try meditating one day when you don't observe one of the rules. For instance, put on a tight pair of trousers and then try to relax into a meditation! There is nothing like experiencing something like this once to make you appreciate why you follow certain guidelines.

The more you revisit these meditations, the more the locations will come alive for you and the more benefit you will receive from them. You will find the locations expand and become more detailed and vibrant on each revisit as you yourself grow and expand. Different insights will come with each meditation, relevant to what is happening to you at that particular time in your life. However, first and foremost these remain the most relaxing and comforting of meditations: somewhere you will always feel safe and nurtured.

OPENING RELAXATION MEDITATION

This exercise should be a preliminary to every subsequent meditation. It's important that you give yourself that initial time to sink into your inner stillness.

✻ Close your eyes and relax. Allow any tension to seep out. This is your time now, time just for you, to be alone and to relax and unwind. You are now going to release unwanted pressure from your body. Feel it going from your head … neck … shoulders … arms, hands and fingers … through your torso and down your legs … right out through your toes …

✻ Feel that tension you have been carrying with you melting away deep into the ground, becoming nothing.

✻ Now focus on your breathing. Watch it come and go through your body … Feel as though each breath is being taken right down into your navel … Feel each breath as it comes up and out through your nose … Let your ribcage expand on each breath in; feel it contract as you breathe out. Sit in awareness of your breathing for a few minutes. Observe each breath in and each breath out …

✳ Whatever problems or anxieties come into your mind, now is the time to let them slip away. Use your cleansing sanctuary to help you ... Say goodbye to them now ... You don't need them ...

✳ Feel yourself sink into your inner core, into the stillness inside of you. Take that journey inwards now, gently, slowly ... Let yourself go ... Relax ... Breathe into the silence, into the sacred stillness ... Now embrace this wonderful sensation of peace and safety ... Feel it running around and through you ... Feel yourself merging with the feeling, so that you and the feeling are one ... Nothing can harm you here ... You are safe ... peaceful ... still ...

GARDEN MEDITATION

This is another excellent relaxation technique to try.

* After your Opening Relaxation, find yourself in a garden. This is a beautiful place; it is the garden of your dreams. The grass is soft and warm under your bare feet, the sun is shining and it feels warm and comforting without being too hot. There is a soft, gentle breeze wafting sweet scents toward you. You can recognise various aromas of flowers and shrubs, all mingling together. You can hear bird song and the light rustle of the wind in the trees. You may hear a trickle of water and realise there is a pond in your garden or a river.

* Explore your garden. Walk around it. See how beautiful it is. Smell everything. Perhaps there is a wild strawberry patch or an apple from a tree that you want to taste. Enjoy the warm sun on your body.

FIND INNER CALM

You find somewhere to rest. Maybe there is a bench in your garden, or a comfy sun lounger or perhaps you just want to lie on the warm grass. You close your eyes and still feel the garden around you, smell its scents and hear its sounds. You can feel yourself merging with the beauty of the garden, appreciating everything from within.

You are wonderfully relaxed and at peace. Everything is right in your world.

Continue to rest in appreciation and awareness. Feel the nurturing strength and power of the garden around you, blessing all of you: physically, emotionally, mentally and spiritually … Stay in this state for a few minutes longer …

Now it is time for you to withdraw. You have to say goodbye to your garden, but you can return to it at any time in the future. You can resolve to return soon.

BEACH MEDITATION

Try this exercise when you want to transport yourself to another location. Remember to do the Opening Relaxation first.

✳ You find yourself on a beautiful deserted beach. There is no one else there. This is your ideal beach. There may be palm trees waving on the beach or a straw hut. It is wonderfully warm and sunny, just the right temperature for you. There is a cool breeze blowing. The waves are lapping at the shore.

✳ Take a walk and explore your beautiful beach. It is just for you. Walk barefoot and feel the warm sand or smooth rocks under your bare feet. Smell the ozone in the air. You can hear the waves as they fall upon the shore and the distant cry of sea birds. You can see the sunlight sparkling on the water.

✳ You find out that everything you could possibly need or want is here: a supply of large dry towels, sun lotion, drink, food, sun hat, large umbrella, spare clothes, perhaps a good book. Maybe there is a soft sun lounger or an inflatable bed to float on in the sea.

FEEL THE POWER OF NATURE

While you are enjoying yourself in your private paradise, you are also appreciating everything around you, acknowledging how beautiful and perfect everything in nature is. You become aware of the special power of the sea and its pull. You merge your energies with the energies of the sea and enjoy its strength.

At some time during your visit, you are also given an inspirational thought that hasn't been given to you before. Give thanks for this new insight. Take it with you when you go.

Now it is time for you to leave. You must say goodbye to this wonderful beach, but you will be able to return whenever you wish. Know that you will indeed soon revisit this peaceful haven.

FOREST MEDITATION

This is another meditation to bring about inner calm and peace. Again, remember to start with the Opening Relaxation.

* You are walking in a beautiful forest. This is not a thick, dense forest; it is open and light with lots of sunshine. There are different beautiful trees around you and the sun is shining brightly through them, leaving dappled images on the soft ground beneath your feet. There is a gentle breeze blowing.

* Walk slowly through this amazing place. You have never seen so many trees before, a variety of species, heights, colours and shapes. The scents coming from them are wonderful. You can hear the rustling of the leaves and the songs of various birds as they fly through this beautiful forest. There is a humming of different insects as they pass busily by. Perhaps you see a monkey or other wildlife in the distance, enjoying the bounty of the trees. The ground feels soft and warm under your bare feet.

NURTURING TREE ENERGY

You feel the beauty and power of the trees coming into you and nurturing your energies. After a while, you decide to sit down in a clearing in the sunshine. You rest in the middle of the forest, looking up at all the beautiful trees around you. As you sit there, you suddenly receive a flash of higher awareness, a greater understanding about some element of life that had previously eluded you. You wonder why you had not realised this before. You sit in the joy of discovering this new truth and give thanks for it having come forward into your conscious mind.

Now it is time for you to leave. You have to go from this wonderful forest, but you will return another day. You know that you will want to come back soon to continue exploring these inspirational trees.

YOUR ANGEL OF FUN MEDITATION

Let us finish with a light and enjoyable meditation which encourages us to remember the lighter qualities we possess.

✳ Close your eyes and settle into a comfortable position. Feel your body unwinding.

✳ As you do this, realise that a wonderful energy has just entered into your awareness. This is a light, frothy energy, unlike any other you have so far experienced. This energy is bright and instantly uplifting. You may see a sprightly figure as this happens or just hear, sense or smell in your own way.

✳ It literally dances around and through you, making you want to laugh, making you want to smile. You feel yourself relax in the company of this new energy.

✳ This is your angel of fun, come to lighten and brighten your day. Observe what they do. They may clown around or joke and make you laugh. They may just dance in front of you. Perhaps they are singing.

✳ They may be showing you something that you could introduce into your own life to enjoy it more. Observe what they do without judging them. You might think they are silly; you might find them enchanting. It doesn't matter what you think of them, as long as you enjoy their presence.

HARNESS YOUR INNATE JOY

Angels of fun are a delightful boost to our everyday life and can give us a much-needed injection of optimism and pleasure. Do you have an important business meeting coming up or are you dreading seeing someone who always gives you a hard time? Lighten your energy by inviting your angel of fun to visit you, even for a few minutes.

Final thoughts

Meditation is not about escaping from the reality of our earthly existence; it is about helping us to live more harmoniously within it. This means finding out how to improve every facet of our lives on an emotional, mental, physical and spiritual level. When you meditate, you are not being indulgent and spoiling yourself, you are actually facilitating the very process of living.

If you are struggling with trying to find enough time to meditate on a regular basis, when you do next have the opportunity, try meditating on the word 'meditation'. This will give you the chance to rediscover what meditation really means and to strengthen your relationship with it.

Lastly, there is one tool that will help you solve or find your way through any difficulty you have with meditation: the breath. No matter how often you have had the importance of breathing stressed to you, no matter how often you have been told to breathe, it cannot be enough. We all keep forgetting to stop and breathe deeply and yet, when we do, the results are immediately apparent.

Whatever trouble spot you hit at any time before, during and after meditation, the secret to unlocking the difficulty will always be to breathe into it.

You are the true master of your own destiny. Decide you will enjoy this process called life. See it not as something to be got through, but as a moment in time to be treasured, relished and enjoyed to the full.

Closing prayer

Divine Light,

help me to see the way forward with love, light and joy.

Show me how best to help others, as well as myself.

Let me spread your Divine Light through myself and others

without judgement, conditions or expectations.

Amen.